COLLECTED POEMS

WILLIAM EMPSON

1977

CHATTO AND WINDUS

LONDON

PUBLISHED BY
CHATTO AND WINDUS LTD
LONDON
★
CLARKE, IRWIN AND CO LTD
TORONTO

First published 1955
Second impression 1956
Third impression 1962
Fourth impression 1969
Fifth impression 1977

ISBN 0 7011 0652 2

© WILLIAM EMPSON 1955

Printed and bound in Great Britain by
Redwood Burn Limited
Trowbridge & Esher

THE FIRE SERMON

Everything, Bhikkhus, is on fire. What everything, Bhikkhus, is on fire? The eye is on fire, the visible is on fire, the knowledge of the visible is on fire, the contact with the visible is on fire, the feeling which arises from the contact with the visible is on fire, be it pleasure, be it pain, be it neither pleasure nor pain. By what fire is it kindled? By the fire of lust, by the fire of hate, by the fire of delusion it is kindled, by birth age death pain lamentation sorrow grief despair it is kindled, thus I say. The ear ... say. The nose ... say. The tongue ... say. The body ... say. The mind ... say.

Knowing this, Bhikkhus, the wise man, following the Aryan path, learned in the law, becomes weary of the eye, he becomes weary of the visible, he becomes weary of the knowledge of the visible, he becomes weary of the contact of the visible, he becomes weary of the feeling which arises from the contact of the visible, be it pleasure, be it pain, be it neither pleasure nor pain. He becomes weary of the ear ... pain. He becomes weary of the nose ... pain. He becomes weary of the tongue ... pain. He becomes weary of the body ... pain. He becomes weary of the mind ... pain.

When he is weary of these things, he becomes empty of desire. When he is empty of desire, he becomes free. When he is free he knows that he is free, that rebirth is at an end, that virtue is accomplished, that duty is done, and that there is no more returning to this world; thus he knows.

This edition includes all the verse in *Poems* (Chatto and Windus, 1935) and *The Gathering Storm* (Faber and Faber, 1940), and the notes to individual poems in those books and the 1935 introduction to them, also *Letter IV*, which was published as a leaflet by Heffer's, Cambridge, in 1929. I have made a few textual changes. The three short poems after "Nan-Yueh" are my total output during the war years, and acknowledgment for the last is due to an anthology, *The War Poets* (The John Day Company, 1945). The bit of ballad was translated in China in 1951; the Masque for the Queen was written and performed in 1954.

The poems are roughly in the order of their writing, but though "Bacchus" was planned and begun in Japan in 1933 the middle parts of it only got finished in China in 1939, so by the time rule it might as well have been put after "Nan-yueh."

W. E.

CONTENTS

CONTENTS

CONTENTS

The Ants

We tunnel through your noonday out to you.
We carry our tube's narrow darkness there
Where, nostrum-plastered, with prepared air,
With old men running and trains whining through

We ants may tap your aphids for your dew.
You may not wish their sucking or our care;
Our all-but freedom, too, your branch must bear,
High as roots' depth in earth, all earth to view.

No, by too much this station the air nears.
How small a chink lets in how dire a foe.
What though the garden in one glance appears?

Winter will come and all her leaves will go.
We do not know what skeleton endures.
Carry at least her parasites below.

Value is in Activity

Celestial sphere, an acid green canvas hollow,
His circus that exhibits him, the juggler
Tosses, an apple that four others follow,
Nor heeds, not eating it, the central smuggler.

Nor heeds if the core be brown with maggots' raven,
Dwarf seeds unnavelled a last frost has scolded,
Mites that their high narrow echoing cavern
Invites forward, or with close brown pips, green folded.

Some beetles (the tupped females can worm out)
Massed in their halls of knowingly chewed splinter
Eat faster than the treasured fungi sprout
And stave off suffocation until winter.

Invitation to Juno

Lucretius could not credit centaurs;
Such bicycle he deemed asynchronous.
"Man superannuates the horse;
Horse pulses will not gear with ours."

Johnson could see no bicycle would go;
"You bear yourself, and the machine as well."
Gennets for germans sprang not from Othello,
Ixion rides upon a single wheel.

Courage. Weren't strips of heart culture seen
Of late mating two periodicities?
Did not once the adroit Darwin
Graft annual upon perennial trees?

The World's End

"Fly with me then to all's and the world's end
And plumb for safety down the gaps of stars;
Let the last gulf or topless cliff befriend,
What tyrant there our variance debars?"

Alas, how hope for freedom, no bars bind;
Space is like earth, rounded, a padded cell;
Plumb the stars' depth, your lead bumps you behind;
Blind Satan's voice rattled the whole of Hell.

On cushioned air what is such metal worth
To pierce to the gulf that lies so snugly curled?
Each tangent plain touches one top of earth,
Each point in one direction ends the world.

Apple of knowledge and forgetful mere
From Tantalus too differential bend.
The shadow clings. The world's end is here.
This place's curvature precludes its end.

Plenum and Vacuum

Delicate goose-step of penned scorpions
Patrols its weal under glass-cautered bubble;
Postpones, fire-cinct, their suicide defiance,
Pierced carapace stung in mid vault of bell.

From infant screams the eyes' blood-gorged veins
Called ringed orbiculars to guard their balls;
These stays squeeze yet eyes no relief ensanguines,
These frowns, sphincter, void-centred, burst wrinkled
      hold-alls.

Matter includes what must matter enclose,
Its consequent space, the glass firmament's air-holes.
Heaven's but an attribute of her seven rainbows.
It is Styx coerces and not Hell controls.

Rolling the Lawn

You can't beat English lawns. Our final hope
Is flat despair. Each morning therefore ere
I greet the office, through the weekday air,
Holding the Holy Roller at the slope
(The English fetish, not the Texas Pope)
Hither and thither on my toes with care
I roll ours flatter and flatter. Long, in prayer,
I grub for daisies at whose roots I grope.

Roll not the abdominal wall; the walls of Troy
Lead, since a plumb-line ordered, could destroy.
Roll rather, where no mole dare sap, the lawn,
And ne'er his tumuli shall tomb your brawn.
World, roll yourself; and bear your roller, soul,
As martyrs gridirons, when God calls the roll.

Dissatisfaction with Metaphysics

High over Mecca Allah's prophet's corpse
(The empty focus opposite the sun)
Receives homage, centre of the universe.
How smooth his epicycles round him run,
Whose hearth is cold, and all his wives undone.

Two mirrors with Infinity to dine
Drink him below the table when they please.
Adam and Eve breed still their dotted line,
Repeated incest, a plain series.
Their trick is all philosophers' disease.

New safe straight lines are finite though unbounded,
Old epicycles numberless in vain.
Then deeper than e'er plummet, plummet sounded,
Then corpses flew, when God flooded the plain.
He promised Noah not to flood again.

Poem about a Ball in the Nineteenth Century

Feather, feather, if it was a feather, feathers for fair, or to be fair, aroused. Round to be airy, feather, if it was airy, very, aviary, fairy, peacock, and to be well surrounded. Well-aired, amoving, to peacock, cared-for, share dancing inner to be among aware. Peacock around, peacock to care for dancing, an air, fairing, will he become, to stare. Peacock around, rounded, to turn the wearer, turning in air, peacock and I declare, to wear for dancing, to be among, to have become preferred. Peacock, a feather, there, found together, grounded, to bearer share turned for dancing, among them peacock a feather feather, dancing and to declare for turning, turning a feather as it were for dancing, turning for dancing, dancing being begun turning together, together to become, barely a feather being, beware, being a peacock only on the stair, staring at, only a peacock to be coming, fairly becoming for a peacock, be fair together being around in air, peacock to be becoming lastly, peacock around to be become together, peacock a very peacock to be there.

Moving and to make one the pair, to wear for asking of all there, wearing and to be one for wearing, to one by moving of all there.

Reproof, recovered, solitaire.

Grounded and being well surrounded, so feathered that if a peacock sounded, rounded and with an air for wearing, aloof and grounded to beware.

Aloof, overt, to stare.

Will he be there, can he be there, be there?

Being a feathered peacock.

Only a feathered peacock on the stair.

Sea Voyage

Re-plyed, extorted, oft transposed, and fleeting,
Tune from plucked cotton, the cat's-cradle pattern
Dances round fingers that would scratch in meeting
And dures and fosters their abandoned kitten.
Drawn taut, this flickering of wit would freeze,
And grave, knot-diamond, its filigrees.

Pillowed on gulfs between exiguous bobbins
The Son of Spiders, crucified to lace,
Suspends a red rag to a thousand dobbins
And sails so powered to a better place.
All his gained ports, thought's inter-reached trapeze,
Map-sail, transport him towards Hercules,

Earth-bound. Blue-sea-bound, the crisp silver foam,
Forbad be crystal, a lace eringo,
Flaps from the haunch seven petticoats at home,
Wards, silk, in ocean overskirt, her rainbow.
Sand-rope, the sodden goblet of the seas
Holds, concentrate, her liquid pedigrees.
We sum in port her banquet of degrees.

High Dive

A cry, a greenish hollow undulation
Echoes slapping across the enclosed bathing-pool.
It is irrotational; one potential function
(Hollow, the cry of hounds) will give the rule.

Holding it then, I Sanctus brood thereover,
Inform *in posse* the tank's triple infinite
(So handy for co-ordinates), chauffeur
The girdered sky, and need not dive in it;

Stand, wolf-chased Phoebus, ϕ infinite-reined,
Aton of maggots of reflected girder
(Steeds that on Jonah a grim start have gained)
And need not keep the moment, nor yet murder.

Crashing and gay, musical and shocking,
They (green for hares) however, tear me down,
Rut or retract, by gulf or rocks. Menacing,
Assuring, their tin reverberant town

"Thicker than water" (cleaned out before solid)
Agglutinate, whose wounds raw air composes,
Shall clot (already has forewarned with olive
These doves undriven that coo, Ark neuroses)

Unless, in act, to turbulence, discerning
His shade, not image, on smashed glass disbanded,
One, curve and pause, conscious of strain of turning
Only (muscle on bone, the rein cone now handed)

Unchart the second, the obstetric, chooses,
Leaves isle equation by not frozen ford,
And, to break scent, under foamed new phusis
Dives to receive in memory reward.

Fall to them, Lucifer, Sun's Son. Splash high
Jezebel. Throw her down. They feast, I flee
Her poised tired head and eye
Whose skull pike-high mirrors and waits for me.

Leave outer concrete for the termite city
Where scab to bullet and strong brick has grown;
Plunge, and in vortex that destroys it, puppy,
Drink deep the imaged solid of the bone.

To an Old Lady

Ripeness is all; her in her cooling planet
Revere; do not presume to think her wasted.
Project her no projectile, plan nor man it;
Gods cool in turn, by the sun long outlasted.

Our earth alone given no name of god
Gives, too, no hold for such a leap to aid her;
Landing, you break some palace and seem odd;
Bees sting their need, the keeper's queen invader.

No, to your telescope; spy out the land;
Watch while her ritual is still to see,
Still stand her temples emptying in the sand
Whose waves o'erthrew their crumbled tracery;

Still stand uncalled-on her soul's appanage;
Much social detail whose successor fades,
Wit used to run a house and to play Bridge,
And tragic fervour, to dismiss her maids.

Years her precession do not throw from gear.
She reads a compass certain of her pole;
Confident, finds no confines on her sphere,
Whose failing crops are in her sole control.

Stars how much further from me fill my night.
Strange that she too should be inaccessible,
Who shares my sun. He curtains her from sight,
And but in darkness is she visible.

Part of Mandevil's Travels

Done into Verse, with Comment

"I feel half an Englishman already"
KING AMANULLAH after firing off a torpedo

Mandevil's river of dry jewels grows
Day-cycled, deathly, and iron-fruited trees;
From Paradise it runs to Pantarose
And with great waves into the gravely seas.

(Olympe, and Paradise Terrestre the same
Whence, bent to improve, King Alleluiah came
High (Higher, in fact, as Milton boasted) hurled
Clings to the cold slates of the Roof of the World.)

Spears pierce its desert basin, the long dawn:
Tower, noon, all cliquant, dock-side cranes, sag-fruited:
And, sand-born weight, brief by waste sand upborne,
Leave, gulfed, ere night, the bare plain, deeper rooted.

(Herr Trinckler, there of late, reports of these,
A million acres of dead poplar trees.
Well may new pit-heads to wise A appeal;
Our desolation is of harsher steel.)

16

Antred, of malachite, its boulders thunder:
Involve their cataracts, one known week-end:
Then, deep, a labyrinth of landslides, under
The gravely sea, and seen no more, descend.

(It is cracked mud the motor service dints;
Five clays, diluvian, covered some chipped flints.
Tour well the slag-heaps, royalty, we own
The arid sowing, the tumultuous stone.)

Fish of another fashion the dry sea
Ride: can blast through eddies, and sail on:
Can rend the hunters whose nets drag the scree:
Are full good savour: are for Prester John.

(Paradise, like Bohemia, has no coast;
Of bombs and bowlers it has power to boast,
But mail-dark fish, spawned in grit-silted grotto,
Adam comes here for; and recites my motto.)

Camping Out

And now she cleans her teeth into the lake:
Gives it (God's grace) for her own bounty's sake
What morning's pale and the crisp mist debars:
Its glass of the divine (that will could break)
Restores, beyond nature: or lets Heaven take
(Itself being dimmed) her pattern, who half awake
Milks between rocks a straddled sky of stars.

Soap tension the star pattern magnifies.
Smoothly Madonna through-assumes the skies
Whose vaults are opened to achieve the Lord.
No, it is we soaring explore galaxies,
Our bullet boat light's speed by thousands flies.
Who moves so among stars their frame unties;
See where they blur, and die, and are outsoared.

Letter I

You were amused to find you too could fear
"The eternal silence of the infinite spaces,"
That net-work without fish, that mere
Extended idleness, those pointless places
Who, being possiblized to bear faces,
Yours and the light from it, up-buoyed,
Even of the galaxies are void.

I approve, myself, dark spaces between stars;
All privacy's their gift; they carry glances
Through gulfs; and as for messages (thus Mars'
Renown for wisdom their wise tact enhances,
Hanged on the thread of radio advances)
For messages, they are a wise go-between,
And say what they think common-sense has seen.

Only, have we space, common-sense in common,
A tribe whose life-blood is our sacrament,
Physics or metaphysics for your showman,
For my physician in this banishment?
Too non-Euclidean predicament.
Where is that darkness that gives light its place?
Or where such darkness as would hide your face?

Our jovial sun, if he avoids exploding
(These times are critical), will cease to grin,
Will lose your circumambient foreboding;
Loose the full radiance his mass can win

While packed with mass holds all that radiance in;
Flame far too hot not to seem utter cold
And hide a tumult never to be told.

Letter II

Searching the cave gallery of your face
My torch meets fresco after fresco ravishes
Rebegets me; it crumbles each; no trace
Stays to remind me what each heaven lavishes.

How judge their triumph, these primeval stocks,
When to the sketchbook nought but this remains,
A gleam where jellyfish have died on rocks,
Bare canvas that the golden frame disdains?

Glancing, walk on; there are portraits yet, untried,
Unbleached; the process, do not hope to change.
Let us mark in general terms their wealth, how wide
Their sense of character, their styles, their range.

Only walk on; the greater part have gone;
Whom lust, nor cash, nor habit join, are cold;
The sands are shifting as you walk; walk on,
The new is an emptier darkness than the old.

Crossing and doubling, many-fingered, hounded,
Those desperate stars, those worms dying in flower
Ashed paper holds, nose-sailing, search their bounded
Darkness for a last acre to devour.

Villanelle

It is the pain, it is the pain, endures.
Your chemic beauty burned my muscles through.
Poise of my hands reminded me of yours.

What later purge from this deep toxin cures?
What kindness now could the old salve renew?
It is the pain, it is the pain, endures.

The infection slept (custom or change inures)
And when pain's secondary phase was due
Poise of my hands reminded me of yours.

How safe I felt, whom memory assures,
Rich that your grace safely by heart I knew.
It is the pain, it is the pain, endures.

My stare drank deep beauty that still allures.
My heart pumps yet the poison draught of you.
Poise of my hands reminded me of yours.

You are still kind whom the same shape immures.
Kind and beyond adieu. We miss our cue.
It is the pain, it is the pain, endures.
Poise of my hands reminded me of yours.

Arachne

Twixt devil and deep sea, man hacks his caves;
Birth, death; one, many; what is true, and seems;
Earth's vast hot iron, cold space's empty waves:

King spider, walks the velvet roof of streams:
Must bird and fish, must god and beast avoid:
Dance, like nine angels, on pin-point extremes.

His gleaming bubble between void and void,
Tribe-membrane, that by mutual tension stands,
Earth's surface film, is at a breath destroyed.

Bubbles gleam brightest with least depth of lands
But two is least can with full tension strain,
Two molecules; one, and the film disbands.

We two suffice. But oh beware, whose vain
Hydroptic soap my meagre water saves.
Male spiders must not be too early slain.

The Scales

The proper scale would pat you on the head
But Alice showed her pup Ulysses' bough
Well from behind a thistle, wise with dread;

And though your gulf-sprung mountains I allow
(Snow-puppy curves, rose-solemn dado band)
Charming for nurse, I am not nurse just now.

Why pat or stride them, when the train will land
Me high, through climbing tunnels, at your side,
And careful fingers meet through castle sand.

Claim slyly rather that the tunnels hide
Solomon's gems, white vistas, preserved kings,
By jackal sandhole to your air flung wide.

Say (she suspects) to sea Nile only brings
Delta and indecision, who instead
Far back up country does enormous things.

Legal Fiction

Law makes long spokes of the short stakes of men.
Your well fenced out real estate of mind
No high flat of the nomad citizen
Looks over, or train leaves behind.

Your rights extend under and above your claim
Without bound; you own land in Heaven and Hell;
Your part of earth's surface and mass the same,
Of all cosmos' volume, and all stars as well.

Your rights reach down where all owners meet, in Hell's
Pointed exclusive conclave, at earth's centre
(Your spun farm's root still on that axis dwells);
And up, through galaxies, a growing sector.

You are nomad yet; the lighthouse beam you own
Flashes, like Lucifer, through the firmament.
Earth's axis varies; your dark central cone
Wavers, a candle's shadow, at the end.

Sleeping out in a College Cloister

Stevenson says they wake at two o'clock
Who lie with Earth, when the birds wake, and sigh;
Turn over, as does she, once in the night;
Breathe and consider what this quiet is,
Conscious of sleep a moment, and the stars.
But it's about then one stamped on someone
And chose an animate basis for one's mattress,
It must be later you look round and notice
The ground plan has been narrowed and moved up;
How much more foliage appears by star-light;
That Hall shelters at night under the trees.
 Earth at a decent distance is the Globe
(One has seen them smaller); within a hundred miles
She's *terra firma*, you look down to her.
There is a nightmare period between
(As if it were a thing you had to swallow)
When it engulfs the sky, and remains alien,
When the full size of the thing coming upon you
Rapes the mind, and will not be unimagined.
The creepiness of Cambridge scenery,
In the same way, consists in having trees,
And never, from any view-point, looking "wooded"—
What was once virgin forest, in safe hands.
 But here the opposite disorder charms;
What was planned as airy and wide open space
Grown cramped, seem stifled here under traditions,
(Traditor), their chosen proportions lost;
Here jungle re-engulfs palace and campus;

The "*high* hall garden" of Lawn-Tennyson
(This is the uncomfortable view of night)
Drowned under flounces and bell-calm of trees.

Earth has Shrunk in the Wash

They pass too fast. Ships, and there's time for sighing;
Express and motor, Doug can jump between.
Only dry earth now asteroid her flying
Mates, if they miss her, must flick past unseen;

Or striking breasts that once the air defended
(Bubble of rainbow straddling between twilights,
Mother-of-pearl that with earth's oyster ended)
They crash and burrow and spill all through skylights.

There, airless now, from the bare sun take cancer,
Curve spines as earth and gravitation wane,
Starve on the mirror images of plants, or
Miss diabeatic down odd carbon chain.

One daily tortures the poor Christ anew
(On every planet moderately true)
But has much more to do,
And can so much entail here,
Daily brings rabbits to a new Australia,
New unforeseen, new cataclysmic failure,

And cannot tell. He who all answers brings
May (ever in the great taskmaster's eye)
Dowser be of his candle as of springs,
And pump the valley with the tunnel dry.

Flighting for Duck

Egyptian banks, an avenue of clay,
Define the drain between constructed marshes
(Two silted lakes, silver and brown, with grass,
Without background, far from hills, at evening).
Its pomp makes a high road between their sheets
(Mud shoals, a new alluvium, dabbled water,
Shallow, and specked with thistles, not yet mastered)
At the subdued triumph of whose end
Two transept banks, the castle guard, meet it,
Screening the deeper water they surround
With even line of low but commanding pinetrees
Dark but distinguished as a row of peacocks.
The darker silhouette is where a barn
Straddling two banks over a lesser channel
Stands pillared upon treetrunks like a guildhall
Empty, mudheaped, through which the alluvial scheme
Flows temporary as the modern world.
The mud's tough glue is drying our still feet.
A mild but powerful flow moves through the flats
Laden with soil to feed the further warping.

"What was that drumming in the sky? What cry
Squawked from the rustled rushes a reply?
Was it near? Are they coming?
Could you hear?" Sound travels a good way by night;
That farm dog barking's half a mile away.
But when the swarms gathering for food repay us
This hint of anti-aircraft is disarmed
And as the fleets at a shot reascend

The eye orders their unreachable chaos
(The stars are moving like these duck, but slower,
Sublime, their tails absurd, their voices harsh)
And analyses into groups the crowds.
Two surfaces of birds, higher and lower,
Rise up and cross each other and distend
As one flight to the river turns, alarmed.
They are out of shot, and like the turning clouds
From meditative cigarettes amuse,
Manure in smoke over the fructuant marsh,
Curled vapour, incense from the cult of Ouse.

Bang. Bang. Two duck blur 'mid the social crew;
For man created, to man's larder due.
With plump or splash on the new-nurtured field
To Reason's arm they proper homage yield.
"The well-taught dogs wait but the voice to run,
Eager, and conscious of the murd'ring gun."

Starlit, mistcircled, one whole pearl embrowned,
An even dusked silver of earth and sky
Held me, dazzled with cobwebs, staring round.
The black band of my hat leapt to my eye.
Alone in sight not coloured like the ground
It lit, like a struck match, everything by.

Letter III

Re-edify me, moon, give me again
My undetailed order, the designer's sketches.
Strong from your beams I can sustain the sun's
That discompose me to disparate pain.
Your vast reflection from that altar runs
But "o'er the dark her silver mantle" stretches;
Boxed, therefore, in your cedar, my cigarette
Kept moist, and with borrowed fragrance, may do yet.

My pleasure in the simile thins.
The moon's softness makes deep velvet of shadows;
Only lightning beats it for the lace of Gothic
On parties waiting for romance of ruins.
No lunacy, no re-imagined flick
The full relief your restoration glows.
On my each face you a full sky unfurl;
You heal the blind into a round of pearl.

"When sleepless lovers, just at twelve, awake"
(God made such light, before sun or focus, shine)
I, nightmare past, in sane day take no harm,
(Passed too the cold bitter pallor of day-break),
And diffused shadowless daylight of your calm
Empties its heaven into my square garish sky-sign.
These then your crowns: offspring of Heaven first-born,
Earth's *terra firma*, the Hell-Gate of Horn.

This Last Pain

This last pain for the damned the Fathers found:
"They knew the bliss with which they were not
    crowned."
    Such, but on earth, let me foretell,
    Is all, of heaven or of hell.

Man, as the prying housemaid of the soul,
May know her happiness by eye to hole:
    He's safe; the key is lost; he knows
    Door will not open, nor hole close.

"What is conceivable can happen too,"
Said Wittgenstein, who had not dreamt of you;
    But wisely; if we worked it long
    We should forget where it was wrong.

Those thorns are crowns which, woven into knots,
Crackle under and soon boil fool's pots;
    And no man's watching, wise and long,
    Would ever stare them into song.

Thorns burn to a consistent ash, like man;
A splendid cleanser for the frying-pan:
    And those who leap from pan to fire
    Should this brave opposite admire.

All those large dreams by which men long live well
Are magic-lanterned on the smoke of hell;
    This then is real, I have implied,
    A painted, small, transparent slide.

These the inventive can hand-paint at leisure,
Or most emporia would stock our measure;
   And feasting in their dappled shade
   We should forget how they were made.

Feign then what's by a decent tact believed
And act that state is only so conceived,
   And build an edifice of form
   For house where phantoms may keep warm.

Imagine, then, by miracle, with me,
(Ambiguous gifts, as what gods give must be)
   What could not possibly be there,
   And learn a style from a despair.

Description of a View

Well boiled in acid and then laid on glass
(A labelled strip) the specimen of building,
Though concrete, was not sure what size it was,
And was so large as to compare with nothing.
High to a low and vulnerable sky
It rose, and could have scraped it if it chose;
But, plain, and firm, and cleanly, like stretched string,
It would not think of doing such a thing;
On trust, it did not try.
My eye walked up the ladder of its windows.

Stretched in the crane's long pencil of a stalk
(Whose dry but tough metal brown of grass
Flowered its salted down on this tall chalk)
Sole as the bridge Milton gave Death to pass
The beam of Justice as in doubt for ever
Hung like a Zeppelin over London river.
Its lifted sealine impiously threatened deluge,
Fixed, like a level rainbow, to the sky;

Whose blue glittered with a frosted silver
Like palace walls in Grimm papered with needles,
The sands all shining in its larger concrete,
A dome compact of all but visible stars.

Homage to the British Museum

There is a Supreme God in the ethnological section;
A hollow toad shape, faced with a blank shield.
He needs his belly to include the Pantheon,
Which is inserted through a hole behind.
At the navel, at the points formally stressed, at the organs
        of sense,
Lice glue themselves, dolls, local deities,
His smooth wood creeps with all the creeds of the world.

Attending there let us absorb the cultures of nations
And dissolve into our judgement all their codes.
Then, being clogged with a natural hesitation
(People are continually asking one the way out),
Let us stand here and admit that we have no road.
Being everything, let us admit that is to be something,
Or give ourselves the benefit of the doubt;
Let us offer our pinch of dust all to this God,
And grant his reign over the entire building.

Note on Local Flora

There is a tree native in Turkestan,
Or further east towards the Tree of Heaven,
Whose hard cold cones, not being wards to time,
Will leave their mother only for good cause;
Will ripen only in a forest fire;
Wait, to be fathered as was Bacchus once,
Through men's long lives, that image of time's end.
I knew the Phoenix was a vegetable.
So Semele desired her deity
As this in Kew thirsts for the Red Dawn.

Letter IV

Hatched in a rasping darkness of dry sand
  The child cicada some brave root discovers:
Sucks with dumb mouth while his long climb is planned
  That high must tunnel through the dust that smothers:
  Parturient with urine from this lover
Coheres from chaos, only to evade,
An ordered Nature his own waste has made,
And builds his mortared Babel from the incumbent shade.

On my unpointed Atlantic where bergs float
  In endless cold: its scream of gulls: the claw,
A Roman feather at the back of the throat,
  Wave-shutter, hanging, flapping, nape and jaw;
  You lay your sunbeam and a part can soar
As tear-clouds, safe beneath their maker, move
In air-ships' gross security, rove and prove
The virgin's fertile lands, Spain-stolen, treasure-trove.

The highest in his bowels (God had come)
  Israel, determined to digest, had striven;
"I will not let thee go," told Helium,
  The unvalenced self-enclosing air of Heaven.
  These risings have more earth-born gas as leaven,
Cheaper, less "bitter in the belly," free
If rain to make but little in the sea
Or if on fire to make too fierce an empyry.

Therefore, my dear, though you can have it all
   As giving goes, the car more safe would ride
Slung on star-netting of a larger ball
   Putting its eggs in wicker-work skywide:
   Stars less monogamously deified:
Who not by light, merely by being far,
Make real Rotational Phenomena,
Prove that I satellite and you true centre are.

Who, being fixed and far, calm and surprise:
   Being no further, shutter and enclose
A rounded universe: who name the size,
   Imply the creature that can count their rows.
   Your sun alone yielding its beauty glows
In growth upon the planet. They are song
Or call the tune to make the dancing throng
Free only as they aloof compose it and are strong.

Doctrinal Point

The god approached dissolves into the air.

Magnolias, for instance, when in bud,
Are right in doing anything they can think of;
Free by predestination in the blood,
Saved by their own sap, shed for themselves,
Their texture can impose their architecture;
Their sapient matter is always already informed.

Whether they burgeon, massed wax flames, or flare
Plump spaced-out saints, in their gross prime, at prayer,
Or leave the sooted branches bare
To sag at tip from a sole blossom there
They know no act that will not make them fair.

Professor Eddington with the same insolence
Called all physics one tautology;
If you describe things with the right tensors
All law becomes the fact that they can be described with
      them;
This is the Assumption of the description.
The duality of choice becomes the singularity of existence;
The effort of virtue the unconsciousness of foreknowledge.

That over-all that Solomon should wear
Gives these no cope who cannot know of care.
They have no gap to spare that they should share
The rare calyx we stare at in despair.

They have no other that they should compare.
Their arch of promise the wide Heaviside layer
They rise above a vault into the air.

Letter V

Not locus if you will but envelope,
Paths of light not atoms of good form;
Such tangent praise, less crashing, not less warm,
May gain more intimacy for less hope.

Not the enclosed letter, then, the spirited air,
The detached marble, not the discovered face;
I can love so for truth, as still for grace,
Your humility that will not hear or care.

You are a metaphor and they are lies
Or there true least where their knot chance unfurls;
You are the grit only of those glanced pearls
That not for me shall melt back to small eyes.

Wide-grasping glass in which to gaze alone
Your curve bars even fancy at its gates;
You are the map only of the divine states
You, made, nor known, nor knowing in, make known.

Yet if I love you but as Cause unknown
Cause has at least the Form that has been shown,
Or love what you imply but to exclude
That vacuum has your edge, your attitude.

Duality too has its Principal.
These lines you grant me may invert to points;
Or paired, poor grazing misses, at your joints,
Cross you on painless arrows to the wall.

Bacchus

The laughing god born of a startling answer
  (Cymbal of clash in the divided glancer
    Forcing from heaven's the force of earth's desire)
Capped a retort to sublime earth by fire
And starred round within man its salt and glitter
  (Round goblet, but for star- or whirled- map fitter?
    Earth lost in him is still but earth fulfilled),
Troubled the water till the spirit 'stilled
And flowered round tears-of-wine round the dimmed
    flask
  (The roundest ones crack least under this task;
    It is the delicate glass stands heat, better than stone.
    This is the vessel could have stood alone
    Were it not fitted both to earth and sky),
Which trickled to a sea, though wit was dry,
Making a brew thicker than blood, being brine,
Being the mother water which was first made blood,
All living blood, and whatever blood makes wine.

The god arkitect whose coping with the Flood
Groyned the white stallion arches of the main
  (And miner deeps that in the dome of the brain
  Take Iris' arches' pupillage and Word)
Walked on the bucking water like a bird
And, guard, went round its rampart and its ball
  (Columbus' egg sat on earth's garden wall
  And held the equitation of his bar;
    Waves beat his bounds until he foamed a star
    And mapped with fire the skyline that he ploughed),

Trod and divined the inwheeling serene cloud,
    (And who knows if Narcissus dumb and bent—)
Shed and fermented to a firmament
    (—May use his pool as mirror for the skies?)
Blind Hera's revelation peacock eyes
    (Before-and-behind
    Trophies the golden throne
    May still be planted on;
    Incestuous Chaos will breed permanent).
Helled to earth's centre Ixion at the wheel
    (He boxed the compassing of his appeal.
    Her centaur, born thence, schooled
    This hero, the paunched beaker, ether-cooled)
Still makes go round the whirled fooled clouded wheal.

The god who fled down with a standard yard
    (Surveying with that reed which was his guard
    He showed to John the new Jerusalem.
    It was a sugar-cane containing rum,
    And hence the fire on which these works depend)
Taught and quivered strung upon the bend
An outmost crystal a recumbent flame
    (He drinks all cups the tyrant could acclaim;
    He still is dumb, illimitably wined;
    Burns still his nose and liver for mankind . . .)
It is an ether, such an agony.
In the thin choking air of Caucasus
He under operation lies for ever
Smelling the chlorine in the chloroform.
The plains around him flood with the destroyers
Pasturing the stallions in the standing corn.

The herm whose length measured degrees of heat
  (Small lar that sunned itself in Mercury
  And perked one word there that made space ends
    meet)
Fluttered his snake too lightly into see
  (Most fertile thief, and journal to inquire)
The mortal Eden forming, and the fire.
A smash resounding in its constancy.
This burst the planet Bacchus in the sky.
Thence dry lone asteroids took heart to be.
So soon the amalgam with mercury
This plumbing: given with it free, the house
Not built with hands: the silver crucible,
Butt-armed: the sovereigns: eats into flaked sloughs.
Paste for the backs of mirrors, there he lies;
Leper scales fall always from his eyes.

She whom the god had snatched into a cloud
Came up my stair and called to me across
The gulf she floated over of despair.
Came roaring up as through triumphal arches
Called I should warm my hands on her gold cope
Called her despair the coping of her fire.

The god in making fire from her despair
Cast from the parabola of falling arches
An arch that cast his focus to the skyline
  Cold focus burning from the other's fire
  Arachne sailing her own rope of cloud

A Tracer photon with a rocket's life-line
And purged his path with a thin fan of fire

Round steel behind the lights of the god's car

A wheel of fire that span her head across
Borne soaring forward through a crowd of cloud
Robed in fire round as heaven's cope
The god had lit up her despair to fire
Fire behind grates of a part of her despair
And rang like bells the vaults and the dark arches.

Your Teeth are Ivory Towers

There are some critics say our verse is bad
Because Piaget's babies had the same affection,
Proved by interview. These young were mad,

They spoke not to Piaget but to themselves. Protection
Indeed may safely grow less frank; a Ba
Cordial in more than one direction

Can speak well to itself and yet please Pa.
So too Escape Verse has grown mortal sin.
This gives just one advantage; a moral Ha

Can now be retorted in kind. Panoplied in
Virtuous indignation, gnawing his bone,
A man like Leavis plans an Escape. To begin

With brickbats as your basis of the known
Is to lose ground, and these ones were compiled
From a larger building: The safety valve alone

Knows the worst truth about the engine; only the child
Has not yet been misled. You say you hate
Your valve or child? You may be wise or mild.

The claim is that no final judge can state
The truth between you; there is no such man.
This leads to anarchy; we must deliberate.

We could once carry anarchy, when we ran
Christ and the magnificent milord
As rival pets; the thing is, if we still can

Lacking either. Or take Faust, who could afford
"All things that move between the quiet poles"
To be made his own. He had them all on board.

The poles define the surface and it rolls
Between their warring virtues; the spry arts
Can keep a steady hold on the controls

By seeming to evade. But if it parts
Into uncommunicable spacetimes, few
Will hint or ogle, when the stoutest heart's

Best direct yell will never reach; though you
Look through the very corners of your eyes
Still you will find no star behind the blue;

This gives no scope for trickwork. He who tries
Talk must always plot and then sustain,
Talk to himself until the star replies,

Or in despair that it could speak again
Assume what answers any wits have found
In evening dress on rafts upon the main,
Not therefore uneventful or soon drowned.

Aubade

Hours before dawn we were woken by the quake.
My house was on a cliff. The thing could take
Bookloads off shelves, break bottles in a row.
Then the long pause and then the bigger shake.
It seemed the best thing to be up and go.

And far too large for my feet to step by.
I hoped that various buildings were brought low.
The heart of standing is you cannot fly.

It seemed quite safe till she got up and dressed.
The guarded tourist makes the guide the test.
Then I said The Garden? Laughing she said No.
Taxi for her and for me healthy rest.
It seemed the best thing to be up and go.

The language problem but you have to try.
Some solid ground for lying could she show?
The heart of standing is you cannot fly.

None of these deaths were her point at all.
The thing was that being woken he would bawl
And finding her not in earshot he would know.
I tried saying Half an Hour to pay this call.
It seemed the best thing to be up and go.

I slept, and blank as that I would yet lie.
Till you have seen what a threat holds below,
The heart of standing is you cannot fly.

Tell me again about Europe and her pains,
Who's tortured by the drought, who by the rains.
Glut me with floods where only the swine can row
Who cuts his throat and let him count his gains.
It seemed the best thing to be up and go.

A bedshift flight to a Far Eastern sky.
Only the same war on a stronger toe.
The heart of standing is you cannot fly.

Tell me more quickly what I lost by this,
Or tell me with less drama what they miss
Who call no die a god for a good throw,
Who say after two aliens had one kiss
It seemed the best thing to be up and go.

But as to risings, I can tell you why.
It is on contradiction that they grow.
It seemed the best thing to be up and go.
Up was the heartening and the strong reply.
The heart of standing is we cannot fly.

The Fool

Describe the Fool who knows
All but his foes.
Wading through tears striding the covered sneers
And against tide, he goes.

Delighting in the freedom of those bounds
Your scorn and even your reason are his aid.
It is an absolute health that will not heal his wounds.
Wisdom's the charger mounts him above shade,

Hanged by suspense and eternally delayed.
"Your eyes are corpse-worms;
Your lips poison-flowers."
They become stars, the eyes he thus transforms.
All the lips' whispers are cool summer showers.

C. HATAKEYAMA [*Trans.* W.E.]

The Shadow

It caught my eye, my shadow, as it ran,
My bad luck, and it had a plan.
Clearly new friends for play
Were what it wanted, since it went away.
I had often giggled when
It dug lines in my forehead,
Or stole oil from my hair to dye its gown.
Feeling it drive its needle through my heart
I had often laughed and enjoyed licking the blood.
You want to please your pets. I began
To fear it was disgusted, since it ran;

Unprepared on laughing to hear rise
Tenfolded echoes, scattering mimicries,
Come from the hills and fields and the far skies.

C. HATAKEYAMA [*Trans.* W.E.]

The Small Bird to the Big

Fly up and away, large hawk,
To the eternal day of the abyss,
Belittling the night about the mountains.
Your eyes that are our terror
Are well employed about the secrets of the moon
Or the larger betrayals of the noon-day.
Do not stay just above
So that I must hide shuddering under inadequate twigs.
Sail through the dry smoke of volcanoes
Or the damp clouds if they will better encourage your
     feathers.
Then shall I weep with joy seeing your splendour,
Forget my cowardice, forget my weakness,
Feel the whole sunlight fall upon my tears.
I shall believe you a key to Paradise.
I shall believe you the chief light upon this dark grey
     world.

C. HATAKEYAMA [*Trans.* W. E.]

Four Legs, Three Legs, Two Legs

Delphic and Theban and Corinthian,
Three lines, by the odd chance, met at a point,
The delta zero, the case trivial.

A young man's cross-road but a shady one.
Killing a mistaken black cat in the dark
He had no other metaphysical trait.

God walks in a mysterious way
Neither delighteth he in any man's legs.

The wrecked girl, still raddled with Napoleon's paint,
Nose eaten by a less clear conqueror,
Still orientated to the average dawn,
Behind, Sahara, before, Nile and man
A toy abandoned, sure, after so many,
That the next sun will take her for a walk,
Still lifts a touching dog's face eager for a sign.

Not one for generalising his solutions
Oedipus placed the riddle with a name.
Another triumph for the commonplace.
While too much to pretend she fell and burst
It is a comfort that the Sphinx took such an answer.

Reflection from Rochester

"But wretched Man is still in arms for Fear."

"From fear to fear, successively betrayed"—
By making risks to give a cause for fear
(Feeling safe with causes, and from birth afraid),

By climbing higher not to look down, by mere
Destruction of the accustomed because strange
(Too complex a loved system, or too clear),

By needing change but not too great a change
And therefore a new fear—man has achieved
All the advantage of a wider range,

Successfully has the first fear deceived,
Thought the wheels run on sleepers. This is not
The law of nature it has been believed.

Increasing power (it has increased a lot)
Embarrasses "attempted suicides,"
Narrows their margin. Policies that got

"Virility from war" get much besides;
The mind, as well in mining as in gas
War's parallel, now less easily decides

On a good root-confusion to amass
Much safety from irrelevant despair.
Mere change in numbers made the process crass.

We now turn blank eyes for a pattern there
Where first the race of armament was made;
Where a less involute compulsion played.
"For hunger or for love they bite and tear."

Courage means Running

Fearful "had the root of the matter," bringing
Him things to fear, and he read well that ran;
Muchafraid went over the river singing

Though none knew what she sang. Usual for a man
Of Bunyan's courage to respect fear. It is the two
Most exquisite surfaces of knowledge can

Get clap (the other is the eye). Steadily you
Should clean your teeth, for your own weapon's near
Your own throat always. No purpose, view,

Or song but's weak if without the ballast of fear.
We fail to hang on those firm times that met
And knew a fear because when simply here

It does not suggest its transformation. Yet
To escape emotion (a common hope) and attain
Cold truth is essentially to get

Out by a rival emotion fear. We gain
Truth, to put it sanely, by gift of pleasure
And courage, but, since pleasure knits with pain,

Both presume fear. To take fear as the measure
May be a measure of self-respect. Indeed
As the operative clue in seeking treasure

Is normally trivial and the urgent creed
To balance enough possibles; as both bard
And hack must blur or peg lest you misread;

As to be hurt is petty, and to be hard
Stupidity; as the economists raise
Bafflement to a boast we all take as guard;

As the flat patience of England is a gaze
Over the drop, and "high" policy means clinging;
There is not much else that we dare to praise.

Ignorance of Death

Then there is this civilising love of death, by which
Even music and painting tell you what else to love.
Buddhists and Christians contrive to agree about death

Making death their ideal basis for different ideals.
The Communists however disapprove of death
Except when practical. The people who dig up

Corpses and rape them are I understand not reported.
The Freudians regard the death-wish as fundamental,
Though "the clamour of life" proceeds from its rival "Eros."

Whether you are to admire a given case for making less
    clamour
Is not their story. Liberal hopefulness
Regards death as a mere border to an improving picture.

Because we have neither hereditary nor direct knowledge of
    death
It is the trigger of the literary man's biggest gun
And we are happy to equate it to any conceived calm.

Heaven me, when a man is ready to die about something
Other than himself, and is in fact ready because of that,
Not because of himself, that is something clear about himself.

Otherwise I feel very blank upon this topic,
And think that though important, and proper for anyone to
    bring up,
It is one that most people should be prepared to be blank upon.

Slowly the poison the whole blood stream fills.
It is not the effort nor the failure tires.
The waste remains, the waste remains and kills.

It is not your system or clear sight that mills
Down small to the consequence a life requires;
Slowly the poison the whole blood stream fills.

They bled an old dog dry yet the exchange rills
Of young dog blood gave but a month's desires
The waste remains, the waste remains and kills.

It is the Chinese tombs and the slag hills
Usurp the soil, and not the soil retires.
Slowly the poison the whole blood stream fills.

Not to have fire is to be a skin that shrills.
The complete fire is death. From partial fires
The waste remains, the waste remains and kills.

It is the poems you have lost, the ills
From missing dates, at which the heart expires.
Slowly the poison the whole blood stream fills.
The waste remains, the waste remains and kills.

Success

I have mislaid the torment and the fear.
You should be praised for taking them away.
Those that doubt drugs, let them doubt which was here.

Well are they doubted for they turn out dear.
I feed on flatness and am last to leave.
Verse likes despair. Blame it upon the beer
I have mislaid the torment and the fear.

All losses haunt us. It was a reprieve
Made Dostoevsky talk out queer and clear.

Those stay most haunting that most soon deceive

And turn out no loss of the various Zoo
The public spirits or the private play.
Praised once for having taken these away
What is it else then such a thing can do?

Lose is Find with great marsh lights like you.
Those that doubt drugs, let them doubt which was here
When this leaves the green afterlight of day.
Nor they nor I know what we shall believe.
You should be praised for taking them away.

Waiting for the end, boys, waiting for the end.
What is there to be or do?
What's become of me or you?
Are we kind or are we true?
Sitting two and two, boys, waiting for the end.

Shall I build a tower, boys, knowing it will rend
Crack upon the hour, boys, waiting for the end?
Shall I pluck a flower, boys, shall I save or spend?
All turns sour, boys, waiting for the end.

Shall I send a wire, boys? Where is there to send?
All are under fire, boys, waiting for the end.
Shall I turn a sire, boys? Shall I choose a friend?
The fat is in the pyre, boys, waiting for the end.

Shall I make it clear, boys, for all to apprehend,
Those that will not hear, boys, waiting for the end,
Knowing it is near, boys, trying to pretend,
Sitting in cold fear, boys, waiting for the end?

Shall we send a cable, boys, accurately penned,
Knowing we are able, boys, waiting for the end,
Via the Tower of Babel, boys? Christ will not ascend.
He's hiding in his stable, boys, waiting for the end.

Shall we blow a bubble, boys, glittering to distend,
Hiding from our trouble, boys, waiting for the end?
When you build on rubble, boys, Nature will append
Double and re-double, boys, waiting for the end.

Shall we make a tale, boys, that things are sure to mend,
Playing bluff and hale, boys, waiting for the end?
It will be born stale, boys, stinking to offend,
Dying ere it fail, boys, waiting for the end.

Shall we go all wild, boys, waste and make them lend,
Playing at the child, boys, waiting for the end?
It has all been filed, boys, history has a trend,
Each of us enisled, boys, waiting for the end.

What was said by Marx, boys, what did he perpend?
No good being sparks, boys, waiting for the end.
Treason of the clerks, boys, curtains that descend,
Lights becoming darks, boys, waiting for the end.

Waiting for the end, boys, waiting for the end.
Not a chance of blend, boys, things have got to tend.
Think of those who vend, boys, think of how we wend,
Waiting for the end, boys, waiting for the end.

The Beautiful Train

(A Japanese one, in Manchuria,
from Siberia southwards, September 1937)

Argentina in one swing of the bell skirt,
Without visible steps, shivering in her power,
Could shunt a call passing from wing to wing.

Laughing the last art to syncopate
Or counterpoint all dances in their turns,
Arbours and balconies and room and shade,
It lopes for home;
And I a twister love what I abhor,

So firm, so burdened, on such light gay feet.

Manchouli

I find it normal, passing these great frontiers,
That you scan the crowds in rags eagerly each side
With awe; that the nations seem real; that their ambitions
Having such achieved variety within one type, seem sane;
I find it normal;
So too to extract false comfort from that word.

Reflection from Anita Loos

No man is sure he does not need to climb.
It is not human to feel safely placed.
"A girl can't go on laughing all the time."

Wrecked by their games and jeering at their prime
There are who can, but who can praise their taste?
No man is sure he does not need to climb.

Love rules the world but is it rude, or slime?
All nasty things are sure to be disgraced.
A girl can't go on laughing all the time.

Christ stinks of torture who was caught in lime.
No star he aimed at is entirely waste.
No man is sure he does not need to climb.

It is too weak to speak of right and crime.
Gentlemen prefer bound feet and the wasp waist.
A girl can't go on laughing all the time.

It gives a million gambits for a mime
On which a social system can be based:
No man is sure he does not need to climb,
A girl can't go on laughing all the time.

The Teasers

Not but they die, the teasers and the dreams,
Not but they die,
                    and tell the careful flood
To give them what they clamour for and why.

You could not fancy where they rip to blood,
You could not fancy
                    nor that mud
I have heard speak that will not cake or dry.

Our claims to act appear so small to these,
Our claims to act
                    colder lunacies
That cheat the love, the moment, the small fact.

Make no escape because they flash and die,
Make no escape
                    build up your love,
Leave what you die for and be safe to die.

Advice

Not busting now before the fish away
I would not make such murders of my teens.
I made no purpose of the first of May.
Crash is a cloth but poisons are all greens.

The lovely grass is brown is dry is grey.

The useful sheep feed safely on that shade
Yet rushing on the green one if soon stabbed
Can then go munching on unburst

Nor ask a policy to drown a smell.

The great and good, more murderously scabbed,
No dug-out on whose lawns could spoil no game,
Cosy in bath-chairs and not known to shame
(G.P. came late) looked wiser than we stayed.

Their long experience who all were first
Would disadvise you to say Now is Hell
Knowing worst not known to who can still say Worst.

Anecdote from Talk

John Watson was a tin-mine man
   An expert of his kind.
He worked up country in Malaya
   On whisky, not resigned,
   On whisky but not blind.

He told a friend he felt like death,
   And what you say's repeated.
The manager says "I just sent for him
   With 'Here's ten dollars, beat it

For Christ's sake to Singapore.
   I'm glad to pay the fare.
Just think of the nuisance, man, for me,
   If you pass out here.'

Next day John Watson tapped the door
   With 'Right, take my gun.
You've changed my mind, I mean to live.'
   'I'll keep any gun.
   But I'll keep no madman.'

"This is the funny part," the manager says,
   "He was shot just the same.
Of course I had to pass him to a dickey job.
   Just the natives, no-one to blame.
   But it was quick how it came.
   Three weeks."

China

The dragon hatched a cockatrice
   (Cheese crumbles and not many mites repair)
There is a Nature about this
   (The spring and rawness tantalise the air)

Most proud of being most at ease
   (The sea is the most solid ground)
Where comfort is on hands and knees
   (The nations perch about around)

Red hills bleed naked into screes
   (The classics are a single school—)
The few large trees are holy trees
   (—They teach the nations how to rule)

They will not teach the Japanese
   (They rule by music and by rites)
They are as like them as two peas
   (All nations are untidy sights)

The serious music strains to squeeze
   (The angel coolies sing like us—)
Duties, and literature, and fees
   (—to lift an under-roaded bus)

The paddy-fields are wings of bees
   (The Great Wall as a dragon crawls—)
To one who flies or one who sees
   (—the twisted contour of their walls)

70

A liver fluke of sheep agrees
  Most rightly proud of her complacencies
With snail so well they make one piece
  Most wrecked and longest of all histories.

Autumn on Nan-Yueh

(With the exiled universities of Peking)

The soul remembering its loneliness
Shudders in many cradles . . .
. . . soldier, honest wife by turns,
Cradle within cradle, and all in flight, and all
Deformed because there is no deformity
But saves us from a dream.

W. B. YEATS

If flight's as general as this
    And every movement starts a wing
("Turn but a stone," the poet found
    Winged angels crawling that could sting),
Eagles by hypothesis
    And always taking a new fling,
Scorners eternal of the ground
    And all the rocks where one could cling,
We obviously give a miss
    To earth and all that kind of thing,
And cart our Paradise around
    Or all that footless birds can bring.

I have flown here, part of the way,
    Being air-minded where I must
(The Victorian train supplies a bed;
    Without it, where I could, I bussed),
But here for quite a time I stay
    Acquiring moss and so forth—rust,

And it is true I flew, I fled,
 I ran about on hope, on trust,
I felt I had escaped from They
 Who sat on pedestals and fussed.
But is it true one ought to dread
 This timid flap, that shirk, that lust?
We do not fly when we are clay.
 We hope to fly when we are dust.

The holy mountain where I live
 Has got some bearing on the Yeats.
Sacred to Buddha, and a god
 Itself, it straddles the two fates;
And has deformities to give
 You dreams by all its paths and gates.
They may be dreamless. It is odd
 To hear them yell out jokes and hates
And pass the pilgrims through a sieve,
 Brought there in baskets or in crates.
The pilgrims fly because they plod.
 The topmost abbot has passed Greats.

"The soul remembering" is just
 What we professors have to do.
(The souls aren't lonely now; this room
 Beds four and as I write holds two.
They shudder at the winter's thrust
 In cradles that encourage 'flu.)
The abandoned libraries entomb
 What all the lectures still go through,

And men get curiously non-plussed
  Searching the memory for a clue.
The proper Pegasi to groom
  Are those your mind is willing to.
Let textual variants be discussed;
  We teach a poem as it grew.

Remembering prose is quite a trouble
  But of Mrs. Woolf one tatter
Many years have failed to smother.
  As a piece of classroom patter
It would not repay me double.
  Empire-builder reads the yatter
In one monthly, then another:
  "Thank God I left" (this is my smatter)
"That pernicious hubble-bubble
  If only to hear baboons chatter
And coolies beat their wives." A brother
  I feel and it is me I flatter.

They say the witches thought they flew
  Because some drug made them feel queer.
There is exorbitance enough
  And a large broomstick in plain beer.
As for the Tiger Bone, the brew
  With roses we can still get here,
The village brand is coarse and rough,
  And the hot water far from clear.
It makes a grog. It is not true
  That only an appalling fear

Would drive a man to drink the stuff.
  Besides, you do not drink to steer
Far out away into the blue.
  The chaps use drink for getting near.

Verse has been lectured to a treat
  Against Escape and being blah.
It struck me trying not to fly
  Let them escape a bit too far.
It is an aeronautic feat
  Called soaring, makes you quite a star
(The Queen and Alice did) to try
  And keep yourself just where you are.
But who was bold enough to meet
  Exactly who on Phoebus' car
Slung on a Blimp to be a spy
  I ask before I cry Hurrah?

I pushed the Yeats up to the top
  Feeling it master of a flow
Of personal chat that would not end
  Without one root from which to grow.
That excellent poet's organ stop
  Has very wisely let us go
Just scolding all. He does not send
  Any advice so far below.
But yet this Dream, that's such a flop,
  As all the latest people know,
He makes no leak we ought to mend
  Or gas-escape that should not blow,

But what they fly from, whence they drop,
  The truth that they forsake for show.

Besides, I do not really like
  The verses about "Up the Boys,"
The revolutionary romp,
  The hearty uproar that deploys
A sit-down literary strike;
  The other curly-headed toy's
The superrealistic comp.
  By a good student who enjoys
A nightmare handy as a bike.
  You find a cluster of them cloys.
But all conventions have their pomp
  And all styles can come down to noise.

Indeed I finally agree
  You do in practice have to say
This crude talk about Escape
  Cannot be theorised away.
Yeats is adroit enough to see
  His old word Dream must now leave play
For dreams in quite another shape,
  And Freud, and that his word can stay.
That force and breadth of mind all we
  Can't hope for, whether bleak or gay;
We put his soundings down on tape
  And mark where others went astray.
So dreams it may be right to flee,
  And as to fleeing, that we may.

So far I seem to have forgot
  About the men who really soar.
We think about them quite a bit;
  Elsewhere there's reason to think more.
With Ministers upon the spot
  (Driven a long way from the War)
And training camps, the place is fit
  For bombs. The railway was the chore
Next town. The thing is, they can not
  Take aim. Two hundred on one floor
Were wedding guests cleverly hit
  Seven times and none left to deplore.

Politics are what verse should
  Not fly from, or it goes all wrong.
I feel the force of that all right,
  And had I speeches they were song.
But really, does it do much good
  To put in verse however strong
The welter of a doubt at night
  At home, in which I too belong?
The heat-mists that my vision hood
  Shudder precisely with the throng.
England I think an eagle flight
  May come too late, may take too long.
What would I teach it? Where it could
  The place has answered like a gong.

What are these things I do not face,
  The reasons for entire despair,

Trenching the map into the lines
    That prove no building can be square?
Not nationalism nor yet race
    Poisons the mind, poisons the air,
Excuses, consequences, signs,
    But not the large thing that is there.
Real enough to keep a place
    Like this from owning its new heir;
But economics are divines,
    They have the floor, they have the flair. . . .

Revolt and mercy fired no sparks
    In the Red argument at all;
Only what all of us desire,
    That the whole system should not stall.
The real impressiveness of Marx
    Lay in combining a high call
With what seemed proof that certain fire
    Attended all who joined with Saul.
Stalin amended his remarks
    By saying they would not fall
But must be trod into the mire
    (And till his baby state could crawl
It must not venture on such larks).
    This let them back against a wall.

The tedious triumphs of the mind
    Are more required than some suppose
To make a destiny absurd
    And dung a desert for a rose.

It seems unpleasantly refined
    To put things off till someone knows.
Economists have got the bird
    And dignity and high repose.
One asked me twenty years to find
    The thread to where the monster grows.
But we wait upon the word
    They may too late or not disclose.

"This passive style might pass perhaps
    Squatting in England with the beer.
But if that's all you think of, what
    In God's name are you doing here?
If economics sent the Japs
    They have the rudder that will steer;
Pretence of sympathy is not
    So rare it pays you for a tear.
Hark at these Germans, hopeful chaps,
    Who mean to split the country dear."
It is more hopeful on the spot.
    The "News," the conferences that leer,
The creeping fog, the civil traps,
    These are what force you into fear.

Besides, you aren't quite good for nowt
    Or clinging wholly as a burr
Replacing men who must get out,
    Nor is it shameful to aver
A vague desire to be about
    Where the important things occur . . .

And no desire at all to tout
　　About how blood strokes down my fur—
We have a Pandarus school of trout
　　That hangs round battles just to purr—
The Golden Bough, you needn't doubt,
　　"Are crucifixions what they were?" . . .

　　　　　　．　　　．　　　．

I said I wouldn't fly again
　　For quite a bit. I did not know.
Even in breathing tempest-tossed,
　　Scattering to winnow and to sow,
With convolutions for a brain,
　　Man moves, and we have got to go.
Claiming no heavy personal cost
　　I feel the poem would be slow
Furtively finished on the plain.
　　We have had the autumn here. But oh
That lovely balcony is lost
　　Just as the mountains take the snow.
The soldiers will come here and train.
　　The streams will chatter as they flow.

Let it go

It is this deep blankness is the real thing strange.
   The more things happen to you the more you can't
      Tell or remember even what they were.

The contradictions cover such a range.
   The talk would talk and go so far aslant.
      You don't want madhouse and the whole thing there.

Thanks for a Wedding Present

[It was a compass on a necklace with the poem:

Magnetic Powers cannot harm your House
Since Beauty, Wit and Love its walls de-Gauss.
And if, when nights are dark, your feet should stray
By chance or instinct to the Load of Hay
With me drink deep and on th' uncharted track
Let my Magnetic Power guide you back.]

She bears your gift as one safe to return
    From longer journeys asking braver fuel
        Than a poor needle losing itself an hour

Within a *Load of Hay* needs heart to learn.
    She wears the birth of physics as a jewel
        And of the maritime empires as a flower.

Sonnet

Not wrongly moved by this dismaying scene
   The thinkers like the nations getting caught
   Joined in the organising that they fought
To scorch all earth of all but one machine.

It can be swung, is what these hopers mean,
   For all the loony hooters can be bought
   On the small ball. It can then all be taught
And reconverted to be kind and clean.

A more heartening fact about the cultures of man
   Is their appalling stubbornness. The sea
Is always calm ten fathoms down. The gigan-

   -tic anthropological circus riotously
Holds open all its booths. The pygmy plan
   Is one note each and the tune goes out free.

Chinese Ballad

Now he has seen the girl Hsiang-Hsiang,
    Now back to the guerrilla band;
And she goes with him down the vale
    And pauses at the strand.

The mud is yellow, deep, and thick,
    And their feet stick, where the stream turns.
"Make me two models out of this,
    That clutches as it yearns.

"Make one of me and one of you,
    And both shall be alive.
Were there no magic in the dolls
    The children could not thrive.

"When you have made them smash them back:
    They yet shall live again.
Again make dolls of you and me
    But mix them grain by grain.

"So your flesh shall be part of mine
    And part of mine be yours.
Brother and sister we shall be
    Whose unity endures.

"Always the sister doll will cry,
    Made in these careful ways,
Cry on and on, Come back to me,
    Come back, in a few days."

The Birth of Steel

(This Masque for the Queen's visit to Sheffield and its University was a co-operative affair, with the plot hammered out in Committee after an initial skeleton draft by the Vice-Chancellor; additions were well supplied during my absence by the producer, Mr. Peter Cheeseman, and the stage-manager, Mr. Alan Curtis—these additions are in italics. The music was by Dr. Gilbert Kennedy.

The curtain rises on an Alchemist with three minions before a furnace. He bows to the Queen.)

ALCHEMIST Your Majesty, my name is Smith,
      The lordliest name to conjure with;
      Iron all my family made. I'll now display
      A stronger metal, a more brilliant way.
      My alchemy its light on iron turns;
      With phlogiston my great alembic burns,
      Though unsuccessful yet, with Paracelsus' aid
      Today my minions hope to forge a stronger blade,
      For Zarathustra spake to me last night
      In hour of Ashtaroth, by burning light
      Of Erebus. . . .   (holding up a sparkling stone)
      Hic petrus
      In chalybem ferrum transmutabit.
      This long sought stone provides the key you seek,
      'Twill change your brittle iron to nobler steel
      For ancient seekers missed the way of truth
      Seeking to gild their leaden crucibles
      But I, with deeper learning, know that wealth
      On steel, not fickle gold, must founded be;

And this existent stone, their bootless dream
To real profit turns, and does not seem
To . . . . . .
(Minion taps him on the shoulder)

MINION *Master, two black pigeons on yon oak!*
Now let it out! Now let it smoke!
            (Crowd enters and mocks at oper-
            ations with furnace)

ALCHEMIST Ignore the mockery of the hoi polloi;
All genius they hope, vainly, to annoy.
            (A large magic circle is described
            with a whitewash brush during a
            chorale)
Ut ferrum tsansmutarent veniunt
Cum ferro in ignem exspectant
Ut ferrum transmutarent veniunt
Cum ferro in ignem sperant.
            (Sword removed from furnace
            and brought forward)
The time has come to try my newforged blade;
            (A Devil appears)
Upon this anvil let it be assayed.
            (The sword smashes, the crowd
            laughs)
It has failed. It has failed.
            (He thumbs dismally through
            magic book then addresses the
            Queen)
            I appeal,
It is essential that I conquer steel.

Minerva, Minerva. Descend! Only Minerva now
Can save all strength, whether for sword or
   plough.
> (Crowd sings Hymn to Minerva
> as she descends)

CROWD   Hail Minerva (etc.)
> (Minerva descends in a chair and
> addresses the Queen after a curt-
> sey)

MINERVA   Royalty, I am yourself! As you would wish
I now create Sheffield.
> (She fetches from her chair four
> white laboratory coats and a silver
> box. She distributes the coats to
> the minions and finally to the Al-
> chemist)

Be you the watcher of the governing dial
—And you the pourer of the chemical phial
—You with a slide rule I invest
To calculate, design and test.
> (To the Queen, advancing to the
> Alchemist)
>   This poor fish

I turn into a steel technician;
> (She turns to crowd)

And every worker to a real magician.
> (Lighting alters. Alarm clock,
> rack of test tubes and slide rule re-
> moved from box by minions.
> Minerva returns from her chair

87

with large text-book of steel tech-
nology, stilling orchestra and activity of minions)
But not too fast! It is now time to look
With patience on my future serious book.
(She places the new book on top
of the old one. The Alchemist
reads from it while minions act in
accordance)

ALCHEMIST *Massive; pearly glistening lustre;*
Structure undulatingly lamellar, slaty;
In colour greenish grey to near leek green.
Slightly translucent, soft, and unctuous:
Difficultly frangible; and dense
Three times as water.
                    (*He turns over page*)
Dodecahedral structure, with slip planes
In three oblique directions; atomic spacing
One point three six eight four ANGSTROMS.
                    (Final activity to produce sword,
                    music ending with alarm clock.
                    Sword presented and Devil foiled
                    by Minerva. She comes forward
                    to address the Queen)

MINERVA   Majesty, as you know, we spirits are
(through   Diffused, not distant in a star.
strings)   The real magician is two groups of men;
             The hand has worked with the mind, but then
             Each has got both. We need not puzzle how
             They made it work: if they can do it now.

88

(She returns to her chair and the
final chorus begins as she ascends)

MEN   Puddling iron, casting iron,
Is the work of this environ;
And it suits the British lion
Puddling iron.

WOMEN   Blending steel, rolling steel,
That's the way to get a meal,
And we're right ahead of the field,
Blending steel.

MEN   Puddling iron, casting iron;
Send the sparks up to Orion;
Give the Goddess more to fly on;
Casting iron.

MEN AND   Puddling iron, blending steel;
WOMEN   Turn the fire on to anneal
What you feel about the siren;
Blending steel,
            puddling iron,
ROLLING STEEL.

NOTES

There is a feeling, often justified, that it is annoying when an author writes his own notes, so I shall give a note about these notes. It is impertinent to expect hard work from the reader merely because you have failed to show what you were comparing to what, and though to write notes on such a point is a confession of failure it seems an inoffensive one. A claim is implied that the poem is worth publishing though the author knows it is imperfect, but this has a chance of being true. Also there is no longer a reasonably small field which may be taken as general knowledge. It is impertinent to suggest that the reader ought to possess already any odd bit of information one may have picked up in a field where one is oneself ignorant; such a point may be explained in a note without trouble to anybody; and it does not require much fortitude to endure seeing what you already know in a note. Notes are annoying when they are attempts to woo admiration for the poem or the poet, but that I hope I can avoid. Of course there are queerer forces at work; to write notes at all is to risk making a fool of yourself, and the better poems tend to require fewer notes. But it seems to me that there has been an unfortunate suggestion of writing for a clique about a good deal of recent poetry, and that very much of it might be avoided by a mere willingness to explain incidental difficulties.   [1935]

THE ANTS build mud galleries into trees to protect the green-fly they get sugar from, and keep them warm in the nest during winter.

VALUE IS IN ACTIVITY. The beetles live underground (inside the globe of the earth) and are only compared to the crea-tures that may be in the apple; hence to the juggler.

INVITATION TO JUNO. Dr. Johnson said it, somewhere in Boswell. Iago threatened Brabantio about gennets. Ixion rides on one wheel because he failed in an attempt at mixed marriage with Juno which would have produced demigods, two-wheeled because inheriting two life-periods.

THE WORLD'S END. *Blind Satan:* blind like his author Milton.

> He called so loud that all the hollow deep
> Of Hell resounded.

Differential: they follow his movements exactly, as if calculated like the differential coefficients used in forming this view of the world.

Precludes: "stops from happening" and "already shuts." *End* in space but blurred onto end in time conceived as eventual justice—"what there is of it occurs here."

PLENUM AND VACUUM. The scorpions kill themselves when put under glass and frightened with fire; Darwin tried this, but I forget whether it was true or not. *Weal:* the scar of a burn, made as the glass was, the ground still under control of their commonwealth, the circle of the glass rim, and the gain of death. "The veins produced eye muscles to guard the eyeballs from screams." The screaming-fit is supposed to be abandoned by civilised people, so that the machinery of facial expression depends on a central reality no longer present. *Ensanguines:* makes bloody or hopeful. Matter *includes* space on relativity theory, in a logical not spatial sense, because from a given distribution of matter you might calculate the space-time in which it seems to move freely. The line is not meant to be read as anapaests. Then the space not in our space-time, which we cannot enter, is thought of as glass with the universe as a bubble in it. "Novies Styx interfusa coercet"; not Hell but its surrounding hatred is real and a cause of action. The thought supposed to be common to the examples is that the object has become empty so that one is left with an unescapable system of things each nothing in itself.

ROLLING THE LAWN. *Our ... despair:* said by Belial in Milton ("in act more graceful and humane"). There was some advertisement urging us to roll the abdominal wall and thus improve our health.

DISSATISFACTION WITH METAPHYSICS. There was a myth that no element would receive Mahomet's body, so that it hung between them and would appear self-subsisting. The earth's orbit being an ellipse has two foci with the sun at one of them; one might have a complicated theory, entirely wrong, making the other focus the important one. I failed to make a pun on *focus* and its original sense *hearth.* Two mirrors have any number of reflections (the self-conscious mind); a dotted line is used for "and so on." The mind makes a system by inbreeding from a few fixed ideas. Prospero's book of magical knowledge was buried deeper than ever plummet sounded, and the depths of knowledge which had previously been sounded became deepest during the disaster of the Flood.

POEM ABOUT A BALL IN THE NINETEENTH CENTURY. There is a case for hating this sort of poetry and calling it meaningless; I had better explain, to protect myself, that no other poem in the book disregards meaning in the sense that this one does. At the same time it is meant to be direct description.

95

The first sentence is supposed to be said softly and doubt-
fully, getting to normal tone on the last word. The main
idea is the clash between pride in the clothes etc. and moral
contempt for it. *Air:* an atmosphere, a tune, a grand manner.
The last line might look back on the ball long after, reminded by the furnishings.

SEA VOYAGE. The first and third verses are supposed to describe the sea-cat's claws, and cat's cradles are foam tumbling
and sliding back. *Replyed:* bent back, like a sharp answer.
Dures: hardens the product and lasts long in itself. *Abandoned* by the wave its parent, and a wicked little thing anyway. *Taut:* the lines of string in the game would make a
knot, the water ice, the salt a crystal. The second verse tries
to connect the triumphs of man with the forms of the original
sea. Ezekiel was called the Son of Man; it might mean "any
hero acting for, representative of, mankind." Man himself
in the tortures of his spirituality becomes the red rag that he
can hold out, as in making a bull charge, to catch the power
of the seahorses. Pillows and bobbins are used in making
lace, like the lace of the foam; also like webs, making man
the ingenious spider—some spiders fly on a thread overseas.
The sail that gets up a thousand horse-power is the map of
tracks of his voyages, lace because so full of holes; the trapeze
is made of the parallel tracks to and from a place. All his
experience adds to his power, and the earth sails (according
to some astronomers) towards the constellation of Hercules
—not towards a higher god; his origins are still inherent in
him, as his achievements are already inherent in the sea. The
flower *eringo* (I was wrong in thinking the stress on the first
and third syllables) made a frothed-up Elizabethan aphro-

disiac; the sea can only hint by its movement at the powers
inherent in it, like a girl not allowed to try out her powers
in company but dressing at home. To develop its salts into
crystals is taken to be a first stage in developing its powers;
which need to be kept in their place, so that it is like the
devil kept quiet by being set to make ropes of sand. Viewed
as one cup of drink the sea is held in by the sands round it,
from which one could make a glass goblet. The banquet
(soup, fish, meat) follows the order of the evolution of
species.

HIGH DIVE. You can give a single mathematical expression
for all the movements of the water (so contemplate it all in
one act, like God) but this may become impossible either
through its getting more movement or less, from its becoming solid or from the splash and eddy made by the diver.
These are compared to the two ways down from the diving-
board, solid and airy, one of which the man must take; hence
to the idea that one must go from the godlike state of contemplation even when attained either into action which
cannot wholly foresee its consequences or into a fixed condition, due to fear, which does not give real knowledge and
leads to neurosis. A wolf tried to eat the sun in Northern
mythology during eclipses. ϕ is a usual symbol for this
potential function, Aton the heretical Egyptian sun-god with
hands at the ends of its rays; both are connected with the
horse chariot of the classical sun-god. The maggots are the
rippling reflections that show the movement of the water
and suggest cantering horses. Hare-hunters wore green coats.
Thicker than water as blood is in the proverb; I am using
F. M. Cornford's theory that the order behind the "physical"

world was originally thought of as the life-blood of the tribe, so that it changes when that does (there is a fear of society in the feeling that you must take the dive once you have gone up). That is why the water of the tank, taken in contemplation as the universe, is called φύσις and agglutinate and liable to clog. A termite city actually uses dung for its concrete, but a scab suggests creatures shapeless if you remove their shells. The puppy was carrying a bone over a bridge and dived after the reflection and lost the bone.

TO AN OLD LADY. First three words from *King Lear*. *Our earth* without a god's name such as the other planets have is compared to some body of people (absurd to say "the present generation") without fundamental beliefs as a basis for action. When a hive needs a new queen and the keeper puts one in the bees sometimes kill her. *Her precession* is some customary movement of the planet, meant to suggest the dignity of "procession." The unconfined surface of her sphere is like the universe in being finite but unbounded, but I failed to get that into the line.

PART OF MANDEVIL'S TRAVELS. *Gravely*, the spelling of the original, means "of gravel" but suggests graves. Milton said

> *on the snowy top*
> *Of cold Olympus rules the middle air,*
> *Their highest heaven,*

which doesn't fit; the boast was only that the Christian heaven was higher. The Roof of the World is, I believe, the Himalayas; the geography here is as dim as Mandevil's. "Spears (first shoots of the metal trees—of man's use of metal) poke up above ground in the basin of the river during

the dawn; the same spears at noon tower like cranes, and
before night are engulfed and leave the plain bare; they are
upheld only by sand which goes deeper than their roots."
I meant the motor service from Baghdad to Haifa, though
that is far enough from where Herr Trinckler was. The *week-
end* is copied from Mandevil. The *motto* is the King's remark
at the beginning (as quoted in the papers).

CAMPING OUT. The intention behind the oddness of the
theme, however much it may fail, was not to be satirical but
to show indifference to satire from outside. She gives the
lake its pattern of reflected stars, now made of toothpaste,
as God's grace allows man virtues that nature wouldn't; the
mist and pale (pale light or boundary) of morning have made
it unable to reflect real stars any longer. *Soap tension* is meant
to stand for the action of surface tension between more and
less concentrated soap solutions which makes the specks fly
apart. *Their frame unties:* if any particle of matter got a speed
greater than that of light it would have infinite mass and
might be supposed to crumple up round itself the whole of
space-time—"a great enough ecstasy makes the common
world unreal."

LETTER I. The network without fish is empty space which
you could measure, lay an imaginary net of co-ordinates
over, opposed in verse 3 to the condition when two stars are
not connected by space at all; these are compared to two
people without ideas or society in common, hence with no
"physics" between then in what F. M. Cornford said was
the primitive sense of the word. Lacking a common life-
blood shared from one totem (showman because tragic hero)

they are connected by no idea whose name is derived from "physics." A big enough and concentrated enough star would, I understand, separate itself out from our space altogether. Verse 4 describes a similar failure of communication which may in the end happen to the sun; *your circumambient foreboding* is "the empty space round him which connects us to him and which you fear." The *thread* was meant to be "the unlikely chance that we never learn to talk to them by radio and thus find out that they are not wise."

LETTER II. "Which ravishes and re-begets me. The torch crumbles each fresco." *Stocks:* the early race that made the pictures. "The greater part of the frescoes has gone. Those whom neither lust nor . . ." are compared to the fresco situation since they forget. The shifting sand is meant to imply that the cave may fall in and bury the explorer. They have a ground in common only so long as there is something new to find out about each other.

ARACHNE. The caves of cavemen are thought of as by the sea to escape the savage creatures inland. "Man lives between the contradictory absolutes of philosophy, the one and the many, etc. As king spider man walks delicately between two elements, avoiding the enemies which live in both. Man must dance, etc. Human society is placed in this matter like individual men, the atoms who make up its bubble." The spider's legs push down the unbroken surface of the water like a soft carpet, which brings in the surface-tension idea. The bubble surface is called land, the thin fertile surface of the earth, because the bubble is the globe of the world. The water saves the soap because the soap alone couldn't make a bubble. Arachne was a queen spider and disastrously proud.

THE SCALES. Alice in Wonderland, Ulysses appearing to Nausicaa, and the jackal sandhole through which the heroes escaped in Rider Haggard's *King Solomon's Mines*. *At your side* means on the mountains compared to her, first seeming on toy scale then full size; the *castle* is a toy sand-castle, and the tunnels on either scale stand for difficulties of communication; then the Nile takes on the tunnel symbolism as being for long unknown up country.

SLEEPING OUT IN COLLEGE CLOISTER. *Traditor:* betrayer. "High hall garden" comes in *Maud* and seems meant to suggest the long tradition visible in the height of the trees.

EARTH HAS SHRUNK IN THE WASH: thus becoming an asteroid without enough gravitational force to keep its atmosphere. (Civilised refinement cutting one off from other people and scientific discovery making a strange world in which man has dangerous powers.) Douglas Fairbanks jumped from motor to express in some film, but they were going in the same direction. *Take, curve, starve, miss* are imperatives. Under the new conditions man is exposed to the dangerous rays of the sun, once cut off by the air, not made to stand up straight by the tensions of a normal life, and only able to get such food as there might be on another planet, which we couldn't digest. A planet where the food-molecules were mirror images of ours (right hand for left hand glove) would play this trick. I understand that in diabetes your digestion breaks up sugars so that at each stage the molecules have an odd number of carbon atoms, whereas you can only digest those with an even number; you thus *miss* the *beat*; the new food is supposed to have this effect as well. *Dowser* is a pun on putting out a light and smelling out water.

FLIGHTING FOR DUCK. A *warping* is land where alluvial mud is being laid down from tidal river water, by a drainage scheme, for two or three years, to make it more fertile and less low-lying; maybe this word is only used in the part of Yorkshire where I was brought up. *Flighting* is trying to shoot the wild duck that come in to feed on marsh land around twilight. Quotation from a "sporting print".

LETTER III. Quotations from Milton and Pope. True dreams come through the gate of horn.

THIS LAST PAIN. *Her:* the soul, the mistress; *he:* man, the housemaid. *But wisely:* "it is good practical advice, because though not every ideal that can be imagined can be achieved, man can satisfy himself by pretending that he has achieved it and forgetting that he hasn't." This touches Wittgenstein neither as philosophical argument nor as personal remark. The idea of the poem is that human nature can conceive divine states which it cannot attain; Wittgenstein is relevant only because such feelings have produced philosophies different from his. "As the crackling of thorns under a pot, so is the laughter of a fool." A watched pot never boils, and if it boiled would sing. The folly which has the courage to maintain careless self-deceit is compared to the mock-regal crown of thorns. By the second mention of hell I meant only Sheol, chaos. It was done somewhere by missionaries onto a pagan bonfire.

DESCRIPTION OF A VIEW. *Boiled in acid* as in cleaning a specimen and like the process of making concrete; *laid on glass* like the cleaned specimen because of the shop windows at the bottom. *Stretched in* is rather illogical; the stalk of the crane, hanging level over the unfinished building, the beam of a balance, the horizon, and a Zeppelin all "stretch along." *Impiously* because God promised not to send a Flood again and marked the promise with the rainbow; a high sealine would mean that the sea would pour in. *Down* is light brown hair on white flesh compared to the dry grass on chalk downs, compared to the rusted metal over the white building.

NOTE ON LOCAL FLORA. *That image:* the forest fire is like the final burning of the world.

LETTER IV. I left this out of the 1935 edition because the basic feelings seemed to have nothing to do with the moral, arrived at by allegorising Eddington; it seemed sententious. I have tinkered with it a bit since, perhaps making it tidier rather than better.

DOCTRINAL POINT. I meant here to compare together the cope of heaven which protects the earth (a world that seems complete to those inside it, like that of the flowers), the cope of the priest-king that symbolises the protection of heaven, the calyx that protects the growing flower, the rainbow repeating the divine promise, the Heaviside layer that keeps off ultra-violet rays (taken as "freer" than the traditional solid cover), and vaults over tombs under the ground from which the flowers have risen. Also man was given authority over all the creatures, but this involves much toiling and spinning, as when in over-alls.

LETTER V. A locus defines a surface by points and an envelope defines it by tangents. *Knot chance*—where the connection of thought they make possible spreads itself into an actual meaning; pun with "not." *Grit* round which the pearl grew. *Your curve* is the curve of the mirror which makes it reflect a wide area, like a camera obscura, but gives the reflection an odd geometry as in non-Euclidean space, so that you can't imagine yourself inside it. "You make me know about the states though you do not come from them, are not known there, and do not yourself know about them." *That has been shown* by the effect of the cause, as in the argument that there must at least be a structure in the external world corresponding to that of our sense-impressions. *Imply but to exclude* repeats the idea of defining a volume by tangents all outside it. The Principle of Duality states that every proposition of a certain kind about points has a corresponding one about lines; this is supposed to show that the distinction previously drawn was unreal. Pun on Principal, chief and causer. Also "the principle that lovers are inevitably two separate people is the rule of life, and can be made to work." To invert lines into points is to apply the principle; the lines are in part the lines of the poem. And even without this process the tangents are arrows which though missing you may still hold you.

BACCHUS. A mythological chemical operation to distil drink is going on for the first four verses. The notion is that life involves maintaining oneself between contradictions that can't be solved by analysis; e.g. those of philosophy, which apply to all creatures, and the religious one about man being both animal and divine. Drink is taken as typical of this power because it makes you more outgoing and unself-critical, able to do it more heartily—e.g. both more witty and more sentimental. These two = the salt and water sublimed and distilled over from the retort = the sea from which life arose and to which the proportions of all creatures' blood are still similar. Man is the *goblet, flask, vessel* which receives what the retort sends over. Thick glass cracks under heat from getting different expansions inside and outside, and if the flask has a flat bottom, so as to stand up alone, it cracks along the angle. Having to be round it is the same shape as a sky-map or world-map; man cannot stand alone because he is dependent both on earth and heaven. The *retort* is also the answer of Jupiter to Semele, when he appeared in his own nature, burnt her, and begot Bacchus. *Glancer:* she looked both ways and wanted heaven as real as earth. The angel at Bethesda troubled the waters when they were ready to heal you. *Thicker than water:* sea water is a stronger salt solution than blood, presumably because the sea has got salter since we cut ourselves off from it. "Blood is thicker than water," but blood connects us with near relations, as the phrase is used, and this with all life. *Cymbal*—"symbol," *whirled*—"world."

In the second verse a god inside the flask making the brine into drink is Noah or Neptune managing the sea. The point is to get puns for both violent disorder and building a structure—what strength or wisdom the drink gives comes through disturbing you. Noah of course has a reputation for drinking.

Cope—coping-stone and to manage, *groynes*—breakwaters, the meet of Gothic arches, the sex of the horses. The same kind of control is needed inside your head, a place also round and not well known (*miner*—"minor"), and it requires chiefly a clarifying connection with the outside world, e.g. by the arches of the eye, whose iris (rainbow) promises safety as to Noah. The externalised Logos is a sort of promise that the outside world fits our thoughts. Christ walked on the water and the doves of Noah's ark and of the Holy Spirit before creation brooded over it; the idea is that you control the disorder of the outside world by sharing it and delighting in it. Columbus, unfortunate in life, like the Spirit called "dove," once puzzled people about how to stand an egg on its end; the answer was to crack the shell. He is Humpty Dumpty the egg and a foam omelette because wisdom via drink requires breaking eggs, giving up static control; thus making the world go round, like a drunk's head; but he is judge as well as horsetamer—*equitation* is riding and justice, *bar* is sea horizon, drinking saloon, and law court. Beating the bounds was a process of whipping schoolboys at places where it was important to remember boundaries of property; Humpty's wall is remembered because he fell off it. Then the cloud of vapour coming into the flask from the retort is called the cloud that Juno made Ixion mistake for herself. A cock "treads" a hen in copulating, and treading wet mud makes a solid floor. To "divine" something is hardly more than to guess at it, but Ixion produced a divine centaur, tutor of heroes, though he guessed wrong. Getting only the blind eyes of pride on her peacocks' tails he trampled them into stars (on the solid firmament that keeps out the water); hence like the eyes before and behind on the beasts of the Revelation they were connected with both inner and outer and could give truth. For that matter even the passive Narcissus like a dementia praecox case might be seeing the sky not himself in his pool. The error is built into a truth by a wild enough belief in it; and this process though chaotic is transferable; it can get its connection with at least a social "outer world," because other people can be made to think the same. Thus Ixion on the wheel of torture in hell is at the tiller-wheel of the turning earth. I find the poem is giving hearty praise to people like Hitler and Mrs. Eddy in this aspect of Bacchus. *Boxing the compass* is going in all directions but also putting all space in your own box; then *compassing his appeal* is getting what he wanted. Then a settling process has to follow this; the flask is being cooled by dripping ether over it, a process only used for urgently rapid cooling; if the flask is a man he is given an anaesthetic; and the other kind of ether can be taken as the empty space the round earth cools into. As the earth was once molten its firm surface can be called *wheal* as the scar of a burn, as well as "weal" as in commonweal.

In the third verse the fire under the retort is given by Prometheus, who escaped from heaven with the gift of fire hidden in a reed. As before, the violent thing can be punned with a measuringrod for building; Rev. xxi is where the angel measured the city of heaven with a reed. It might also be a yard of the stallions, who appear now under Tartar horsemen, laying waste the land round the Caucasus on which Prometheus is chained. In China it was felt as a major atrocity story that the Japanese had turned their horses into the ricefields, a thing apparently not done in the civil wars. We have got here to the quarrelsome stage of drink, but the god or political thinker who brings it is separate from it and can't control it.

Taught is what he did, but he is now "taut"; Prometheus stretched helpless along the glaciers is compared to the flame clinging to the glass of the retort, and its "quivers" are supposed to eke out a hint at the arches of the Tartar bowmen. As in Shelley he is still helping man by keeping a secret, and drinking the cup of sacrifice (Mark x); one of the vultures at his liver may be cirrhosis and another remorse. Anyway the drink is now chiefly needed for anaesthetic. Aether meant the upper air, and he is fixed high where the air smells dry and choking, like ether. Ether and chloroform smell to me much alike though only chloroform has got chlorine in it, so I swap drugs to bring in poison gas. There is meant to be a comparison between the political case and the personal one; in a drunken quarrel a man tends to forget the cause and get angrier from an internal disunion.

For the fourth verse Mercury brought a thermometer to control the reaction by knowledge, but it burst and the mercury spoilt everything. A herm was a phallic household cult-statue, a minor version of this god, and an aberration of the planet gave the first evidence for relativity. The snakes round his staff were also used for Bacchus, as I remember, hidden under the ivy, and I connect them with the serpent that gave knowledge of good and evil; because in this verse we have reached the neurotic effects of drink; a state of overconsciousness needing continual stimulus from outside, too much of the outer world, as before there was too little. One of the asteroids is called Bacchus, but I assume this is the name of the planet they once all made together, only it burst; the bursting of the retort produces incomplete men, solitary drinkers. These men have their mettle eaten into by mercury, which attacks other metals. I forget what a silver crucible was used for in Stinks at school, but remember how fatal it was to put mercury in; we pronounced the scaly result *amalgam*, which the verse needs; the crucible had little flange arms and seemed an alchemical man via Ecclesiastes' silver cord and golden bowl. Houses are supposed to be given free with the plumbing in America; God's temple was not built with hands. I was thinking of Mandevil when I wrote "so soon," though it would be absurd to pretend that this is part of the poem; he says that Adam was only in Eden for half an hour, "so soon he fell." This paste which mercury makes with metals is used for the backs of mirrors, a symbol of self-consciousness; scales fell from the eyes of blind men healed by Christ, but in this neurotic state further clarifying is no good, though the scales can go on peeling off as from lepers. We have left behind the active politicians but not the thinkers; the non-alcoholic Nietzsche seems a likely example.

After this look-round of the subject I try to present a person feeling tragic exultation in it. *Coping* is a term used about finishing brickwork, as well as for the coping-stone of an arch, and for the cope which isolates and gives divine authority to a priest; the coping of the fire in a room manages it, does not let it burn the house down.

Cast is both "threw" and "made a cast in metal." The parabola is both the path of a forward fall and the shape of the reflector that throws directly forward all the light of a motorcar lamp; it has one focus at the lamp and the other at the skyline before it. Arachne who out of pride against the pride of Juno hanged herself in her own web and became

a spider is here a gossamer spider, who can fly on it. A
Tracer bullet lights in the air to show its path, whereas a
photon though like a particle has no position till it hits;
rockets were used to send ropes to save people off wrecks.
The idea is that the puzzle of the Mercury section about
neurotic self-consciousness (you can't know the position of
a photon without destroying it) has been outfaced. Any
actual car-lamp makes a fan instead of one beam; this is
supposed to bring in "his fan is in his hand, and he shall
thoroughly purge his floor" and "make straight in the desert
a highway . . . every mountain shall be made low." King
Lear says he is bound upon a wheel of fire. *Span* is meant
for spanned and spun. The final arches are cellars underground such as the grave.

YOUR TEETH. There was a toothpaste advertisement saying
your teeth are ivory castles and must be defended. Critics
often say that modern poetry retires into an ivory tower,
doesn't try to make contact with a reader, or escapes facing
the problems of the time. I try to defend it by saying that
there is a good deal of defence in ordinary life (talking or
biting). A critic like Dr. Leavis can speak with the same tone
of moral outrage about an Escapist (sentimental) novel as a
customs official would about *Lady Chatterley's Lover*, say;
but this being over-simple, I was claiming, is itself a way of
escaping the complexity of the critic's problem. The relation
of the artist to his society may include acting as safety valve
or keeping the fresh eye, etc., of the child, and therefore
can't be blamed out of hand for escapism or infantilism.
Then the poem drifts off onto the stock defence that poets
have to be obscure because something has gone wrong with

the public. Our civilisation has been built up on two accepted but apparently irreconcilable ideals, worldly and Christian, and this gives a good deal of freedom—people with different views are still in contact because they are only finding different ways of resolving the same contradictions. It is not clear that in the new great machine or mass societies, which accept neither ideal, there is the same room for the artist. A star just too faint to be seen directly can still be seen out of the corners of your eyes; Max Beerbohm described some hero of the æsthetic movement as looking life straight in the face out of the very corners of his eyes. I suppose the reason I tried to defend my clotted kind of poetry was that I felt it was going a bit too far.

AUBADE. *The same war* in Tokyo then was the Manchurian Incident.

THE FOOL, ETC. I haven't been able to ask Miss Hatakeyama's permission to re-publish these "translations" of her work. My part was only to polish up her own English version, and I do not think I added a metaphor or a thought. Maybe I ought to make clear that she has nothing to do with the Aubade poem.

FOUR LEGS. It struck me passing through Cairo that the Sphinx has a look of pathetic and devoted public spirit (like a good deal of Egyptian work) which makes the popular idea of her as a sinister mystery seem off the point. This made me think about Oedipus, who destroyed an ogre-like Sphinx by answering its riddle, and therefore had bad luck—at least they made him king out of gratitude for this feat, and that was how he came to marry his mother. He killed his father at a crossroad between the three towns of my first line; they seem meant to symbolise three ways of life, rather as the legs in the riddle do. A delta is a mathematical expression for the area of the triangle, here zero; he short-circuited life by keeping it all in the family. A metaphysician (somebody said) is like a blind man looking for a black cat in the dark which isn't there, and black cats are for luck. As Oedipus was wholly unconscious of his crimes it is uncertain whether he had an Oedipus complex, and he answered the riddle merely by saying Man, not by telling us anything about him. Napoleon's romantic paint can just be seen on her face; it is denied that her nose was broken by a deliberate cannon-shot of his. I have never seen anything in print about how dramatically she is placed between the desert and the sown; it seems that she always was, but at one time the river ran close under her paws.

ROCHESTER. The idea is that nationalist war is getting to a crisis because the machines make it too dangerous and expensive to be serviceable even in the queer marginal ways it used to be. However, actually, if you think of Jenghis, Tamburlane, and William harrowing the north of England, it is not clear that the new methods of destruction have yet proved themselves so much more effective than the old ones.* The mind uses unconscious processes (mining underground) and an outpouring of loose words, sometimes poisonous (gas); the reasons that make the thought of a country succeed can be as queer as the reasons that sometimes make

* Here and at some later points these notes are marked by their date, which was 1940, but there seems no need to alter them on that account.

war good for it, and a mere change of proportion might make either fail to work any longer.

COURAGE. Fearful and Muchafraid of course are characters in Bunyan. *Bard* and *hack* I suppose come in a bit oddly, but the point is to join up the crisis-feeling to what can be felt all the time in normal life.

SUCCESS. Dostoevsky had a kind of illumination while waiting to be shot but was brought back from it by a last-minute reprieve. I can't feel that the line about "afterlight" comes off; the idea is that the glow after sunset with its peace is a kind of proof that the day was real or good, and the Will o' the Wisp is assumed to be like it. Doubting drugs is meant to be both doubting whether they have been used and doubting the value of what they have given.

MISSING DATES. It is true about the old dog, at least I saw it reported somewhere, but the legend that a fifth or some such part of the soil of China is given up to ancestral tombs is (by the way) not true.

THE TRAIN. This was when I was going to a job in China a few weeks after the outbreak of the Chinese war. The thing is about a surprised pleasure in being among Japanese again, though the train itself was beautiful after the Russian one all right. What I abhorred or rightly felt I ought to abhor was Japanese imperialism. They have got themselves into a tragically false position, I think; the Chinese with their beautiful good humour were always patient when I told them I was more sorry for the Japanese than for China. MAN-

CHOULI was as big a racial frontier as you see anywhere; I don't remember seeing any obvious 'Asiatics' in Siberia. Argentina was a famous Spanish dancer when I was young.

REFLECTION FROM ANITA LOOS. There is a strong paragraph in *Gentlemen Prefer Blondes* about Louie's spats. Dorothy told him to take them off, because "Fun's fun, but a girl can't laugh all the time." When she saw his socks she told him to put his spats back on. Unconsciously generalising from the fine character of Dorothy, I seem to have taken a very feminist view here; actually no doubt women are about as ambitious as men. The *lime* is meant to be birdlime (also hanged criminals are buried in ordinary lime). I had better say some more about the line, as many readers may find it merely offensive. Anyway the religion of love produced appalling cruelties when made a governmental institution, but it seems arguable that the ideas of Jesus himself got fatally connected under the stress of persecution with the official and moneymaking cult of blood sacrifice, which he had tried to combat. That he drove out of the temple the doves being sold for sacrifice just before he became one is an awful irony in his story. The way earlier societies seem obviously absurd and cruel gives a kind of horror at the forces that must be at work in our own, but suggests that any society must have dramatically satisfying and dangerous conventions; and people can put up with almost any political conditions, either because they are lazy or because they are ambitious.

ADVICE. "Crash" is a pleasant coarse canvas-like material; the only point of the pun is the idea that what seems smashing may turn out quite healthy. It seems the discovery that general paralysis is a final result of syphilis was painful to many old gentlemen who till then had seen nothing scandalous in their complaint. "We" who didn't do much better are supposed to be both people living now, when the disease is more curable, and politicians, etc., living now, who made a smash-up of international affairs though the issues and dangers were clearer than to the Victorians.

CHINA. The two main ideas put forward or buried in this poem now seem to me false, but the thing expresses a kind of ignorant glee which many visitors beside myself have felt about China (about the vitality which lets her keep the beauty of her life however cut up or disorganised, a vitality like a jellyfish, not needing a centre), and I hope that saves it from being offensive. The ideas are that Japanese and Chinese are extremely alike, since the Japanese are merely a branch of the same culture with a specialised political tradition, and that China can absorb the Japanese however completely they over-run her. This common forecast might work out, grindingly, after a few centuries, but does not make her need for victory now less urgent. However, I felt that while I was trying to help China I need not be solemn about her.

The prolonged disorder of China made everything feel crumbling like cheese but with an effect of new growth trying to start as in inclement spring weather; "Nature" is a repulsive deity, but you felt there might be something fertile in this struggle between her two allied fabulous creatures. The ideas of learning wisdom by not worrying and of getting your way by yielding, as in water, of course go a long way back into Chinese thought. The other nations perch about on rigid rules, not using laissez-faire and mutual accommodation. It is the Japanese rather than the Chinese who like being on hands and knees, but I was trying to mix them up. The Chinese coolie still regards a chair as a not very pleasing luxury, and China like Japan has her boat population all right. The Japanese missed the chair, a late T'ang introduction, because they learned nearly all their customs in middle T'ang. You can trace a chair with crossed legs like a folding stool from Mohenjodaro through sixth century Cambodian Buddhist sculpture to a copy of a late T'ang painting, and this probably shows the way the chair came, though not why it was adopted by the Chinese and dropped by the Indians.

The hills bleed in China because the trees have been cut down so that the red earth crumbles and washes away; it is an obvious symbol of disorder. (The re-afforestation plans seem to work as far as they go; I never saw new trees torn out again.) It seems pathetic that the classical literature of China should be interpreted as all about the principles of government, when governing is the one thing she doesn't seem to us good at. Confucius of course believed in ruling by music and by rites. The earliest surviving music is T'ang, preserved by the Japanese, but no doubt the older governmental music felt much as that does; concerned to make you keep your official seat and try hard, with a great deal of waiting for the snap, at the end of a rhythm slower than a heartbeat. Whereas the things the coolies sing to encourage their vast labours (both in Japan and China) are vaguely like Russian folk-music, very beautiful to us and with none of this complete strangeness. A bus is *under-roaded* when the road gives way under it and you spend hours digging in the mud and spreading branches (my friends don't seem to know this word, which I thought was a common one). The grammar is meant to run through alternate lines; I thought this teasing trick gave an effect of the completely disparate things going on side by side.

The next verse brings in again the idea of the separation of the beauty of the coolie life from the official arts (I cut out an intervening verse about Russia, who is an important influence on the country now, because it seemed no use pretending I had anything to say about proletarianism). The paddy fields in hill country, arranged of course to make level patches to hold water, are extremely beautiful, look like microscopic photographs of bees' wings, and seem never to have been treated by all the long and great tradition of Far Eastern landscape painters. And yet they have the same surprising jerking texture as the Great Wall making its way round precipitous hills, and the familiar dragon of the teacups (and by this identity the real line of military or magical defence is the country itself). The whole business of what a culture can become unconscious of and still use is an important and strange one. China from the air is a grand sight, but I meant to leave room in the word *flies* for us scholarly refugees, who were forced to look at the country because we were escaping.

As to the liverfluke, who comes in the *Outline of Life* by Wells, etc., its child does not kill the snail and cannot when fully inside be distinguished anywhere from the body of the snail; maybe it is not even cellular. It only puts red patches containing its eggs on the horns of the snail so that these are seen and eaten by birds. The horns grow again. There is a third generation which gets from the bird to the sheep, and the child of that has to leave the sheep and dissolve itself in a snail. That the thing can play these tricks without having any structure at all is what is so frightening; it is like demoniacal possession. However, to do the Japanese justice, a normal Japanese is still rigidly Japanese after twenty years of living among Chinese in China; no man could be less like this eerie fluke. The idea that China unlike other nations can keep its peculiar life going without a central organisation was the excuse for bringing it in.

AUTUMN. Nan-yueh is a sacred mountain about seventy miles southwest of Changsha; the Arts Departments of the Combined Universities were housed on it for a term in 1937, and then we moved further back to Yunnan. The "two fates" are the opposed ideals of personal immortality and of extinguishing yourself or merging into a world soul; the mountain was a god before it became the cradle of what the Japanese call the Zen sect. Those of the beggars who are too deformed to walk are carried up in baskets and placed along the pilgrims' route up the mountain. "Flying" of course is being used here for escaping ordinary troubles as well as other things, and the pilgrimage is a holiday. The abbot of the monastery on the summit might quite naturally have passed Greats, though I don't know that he literally has done. *Like a gong* maybe reads as rather too easy a sentiment. The claim is that public opinion in England during this decade has been commonly right while independent of its political leaders and the machinery of propaganda; e.g. the outcry over the Hoare-Laval pact and the swing-round of the Trade Unions to rearmament then. Chinese wines aren't drunk except during meals; the point about Tiger Bone was that

I found it made a good drink to sit over when drowned in
hot water. The tiger bones in it are supposed to make you
brave. I hope the gaiety of the thing comes through; I felt
I was in very good company. [1940]

SONNET. This *free* I am afraid only sounds an offensively false
use of the great emotive term, implying merely that the
pygmies and the rest of us had better be "left alone." This
may be true of pygmies, but I was trying to give the word
the impact of a contradiction; as in *Letter IV*, where it probably doesn't come off either. The pygmy method of singing
(on the sound-track of an excellent travel film) sounded
spontaneous though it was a grotesque and extreme example
of collectivism. [1947]

CHINESE BALLAD. A bit from a long ballad by Li Chi, a Com-
munist who collected country ballads during his other activ-
ities. It was written in 1945 in North Shensi, and has since
been made into a much praised opera. This bit was con-
sidered technically interesting because the theme had been
used in classical style, first, I am told, by the Yuan poet Chao
Meng-fu, and was now transposed or restored into popular
style. The translation is word for word, so far as I can know
from simply being given the meanings of the characters;
I added the bit about children, but I understand that is only
like working a footnote into the text, because the term speci-
fically means dolls for children. He crosses the stream where
it turns because it is wider therefore shallower there. He is
fighting the Japanese. [1952]